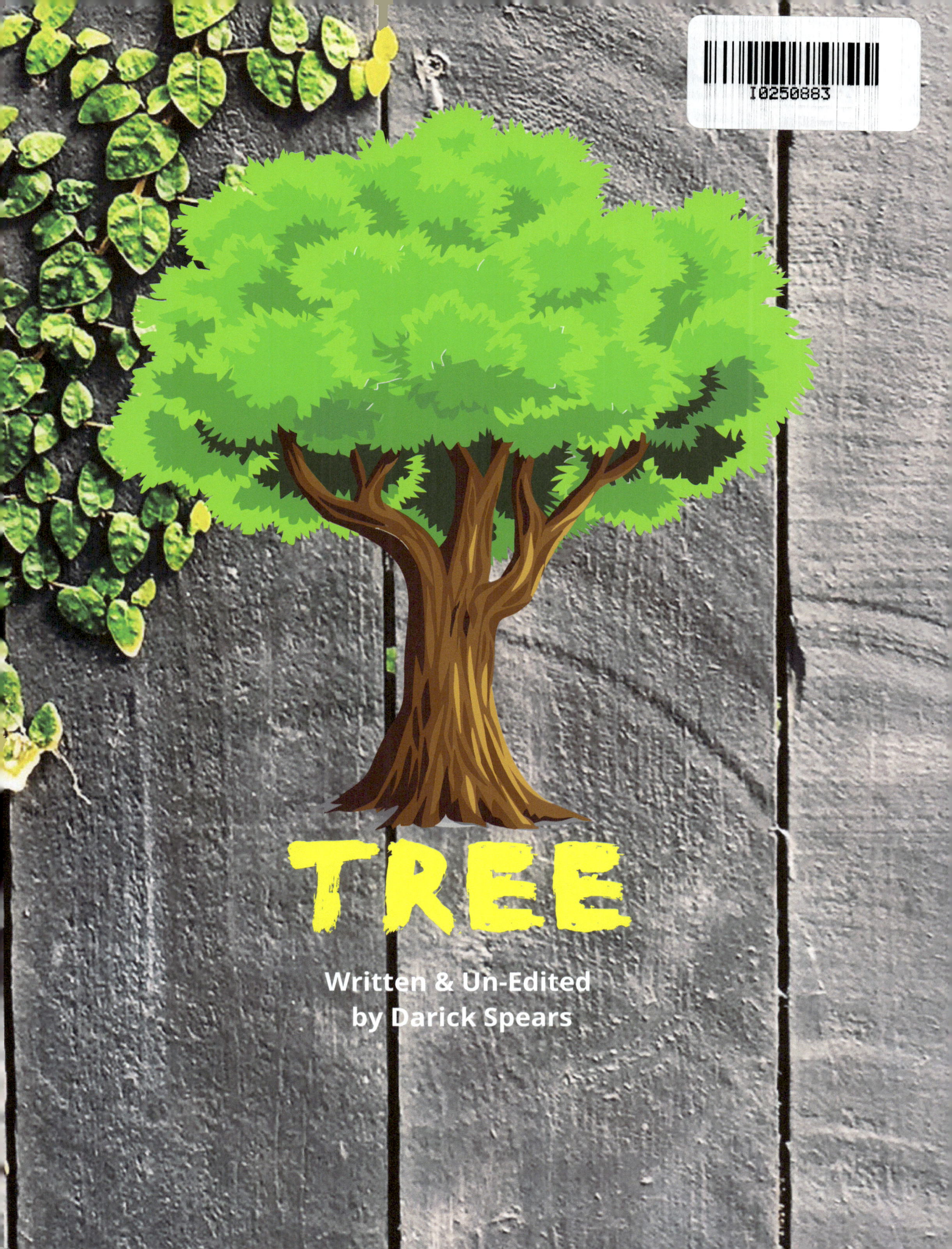

TREE

Written & Un-Edited
by Darick Spears

TREE
ISBN: 978-1-954133-09-9
Copyright © 2020 by Darick Spears
Darick Books
All rights reserved. No part of this book may
be reproduced or transmitted in any form or by any means without written permission from the author.
Published through
Darick Books
DDS Mediaworks LLC./21st Century Shakespears
Publishing
www.darickbooks.com
Get your book written & published today
by
Darick Spears
Email: darick@ddsmediaworks.com
Call 414-988-4946

In these days of hardship, racial and political divides— be like the deep-rooted tree. Ancient and full of wisdom. Unmovable, unshaken, and un-phased. Plant your seeds on good soil, so that they connect with the ground beneath, and their branches touch the skies above.
Be like the deep-rooted tree.

BE FUTURISTIC IN THOUGHT, BUT BE PRESENT.
BE FRUSTRATED BUT OPTIMISTIC,
BE FULL OF ENERGY, BUT WELL-RESTED.
BE YOUTHFUL BUT WISE IN THOUGHT,
BE EMOTIONAL BUT NOT EMOTIONLESS.
BE ROOTED.

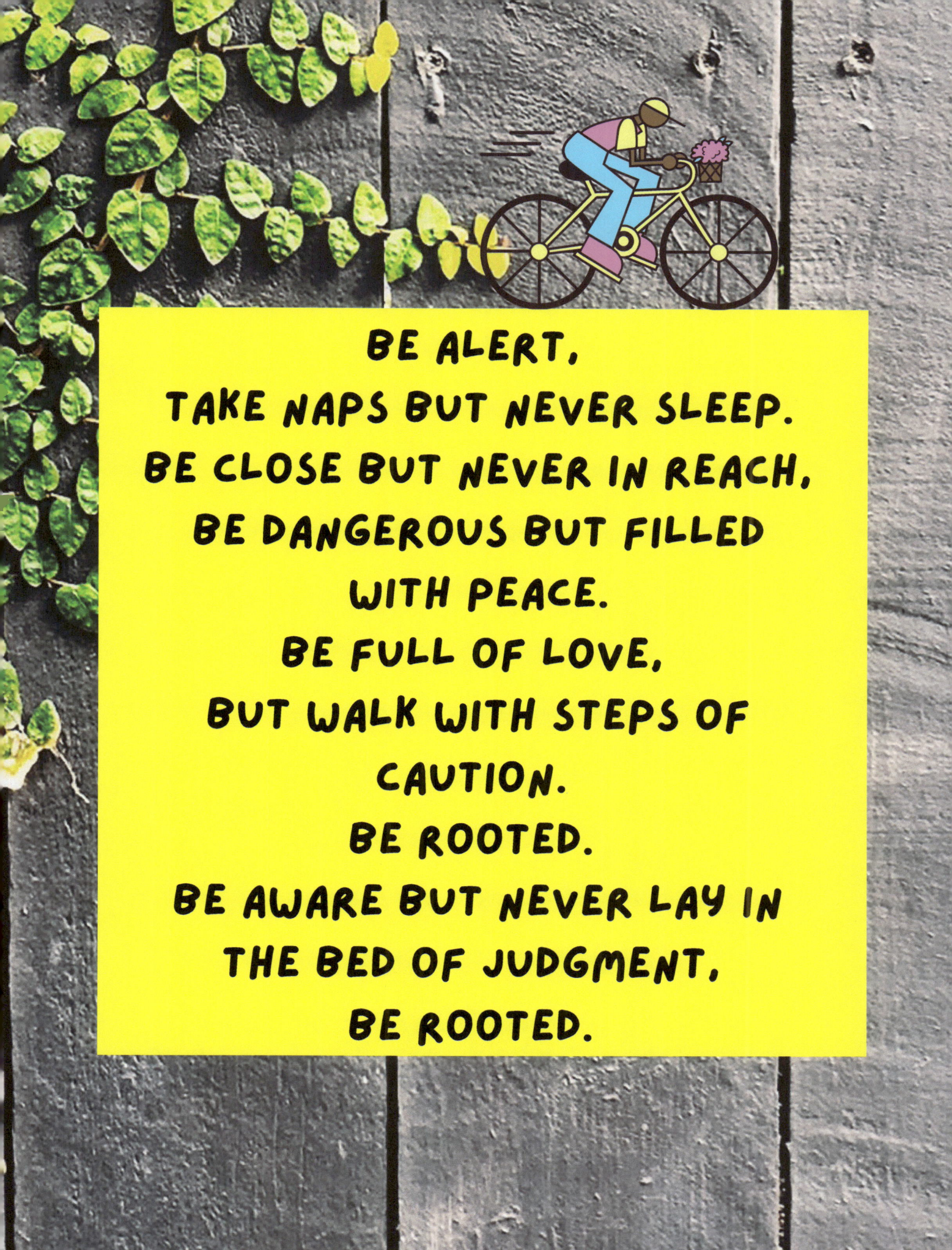

BE ALERT,
TAKE NAPS BUT NEVER SLEEP.
BE CLOSE BUT NEVER IN REACH,
BE DANGEROUS BUT FILLED WITH PEACE.
BE FULL OF LOVE,
BUT WALK WITH STEPS OF CAUTION.
BE ROOTED.
BE AWARE BUT NEVER LAY IN THE BED OF JUDGMENT,
BE ROOTED.

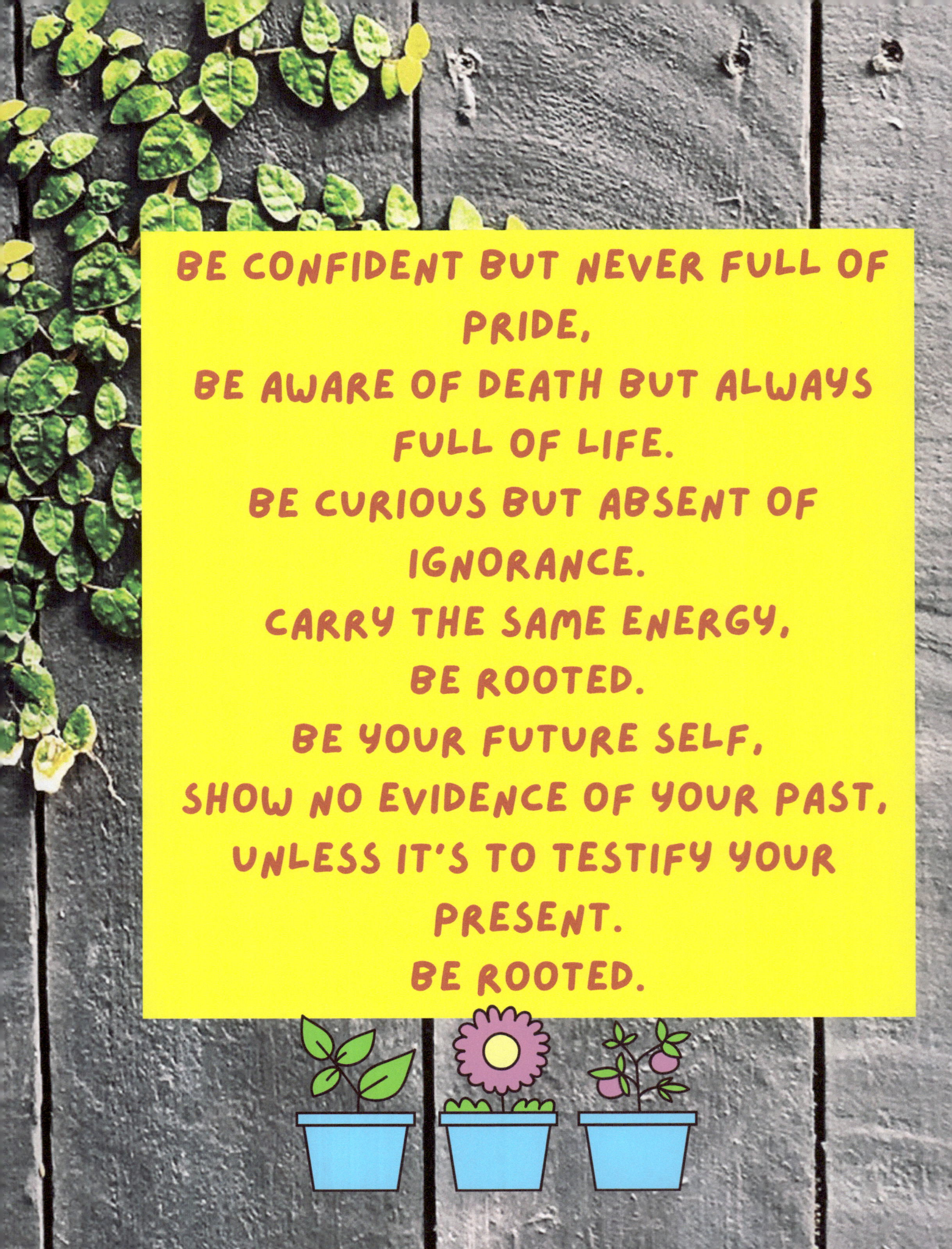

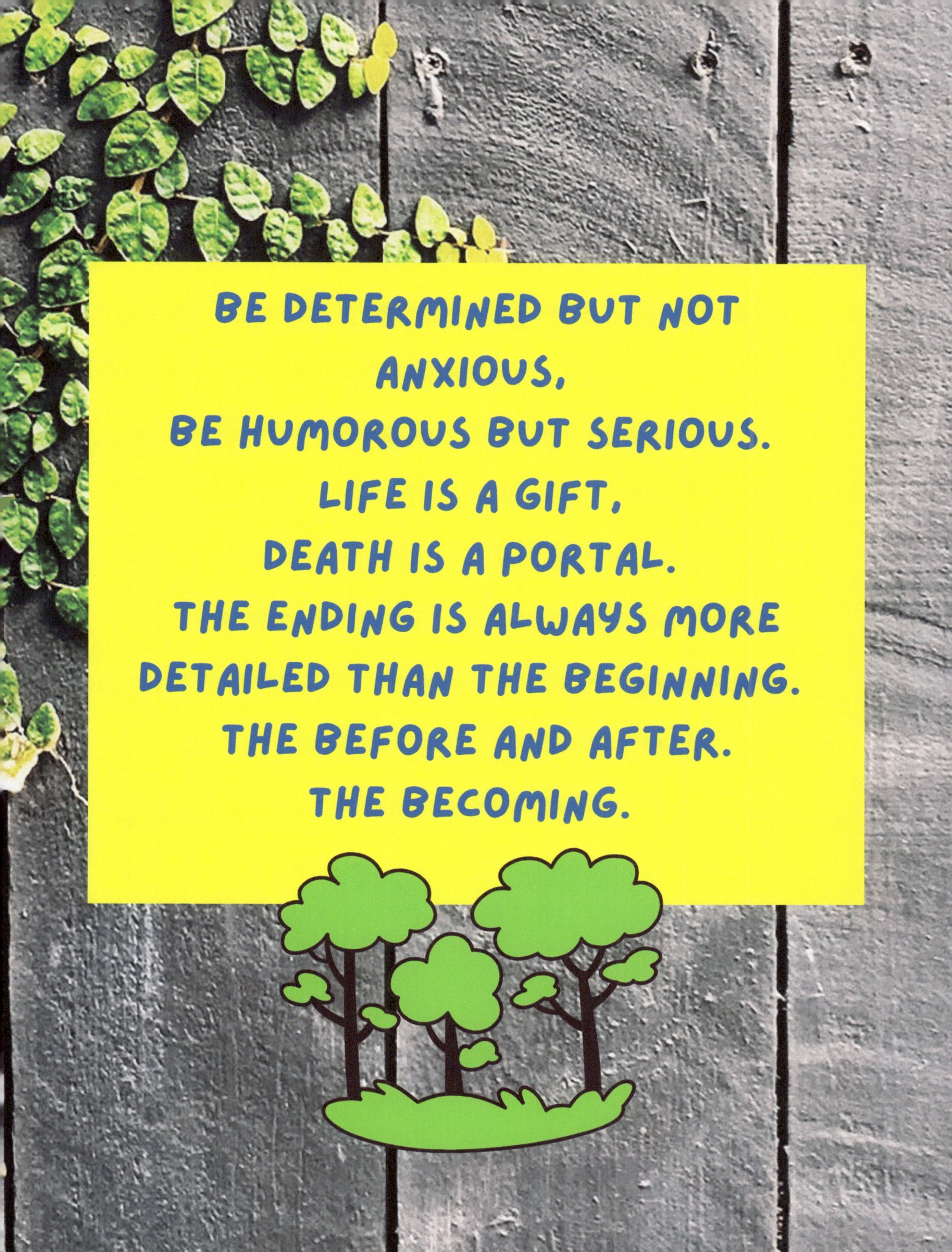

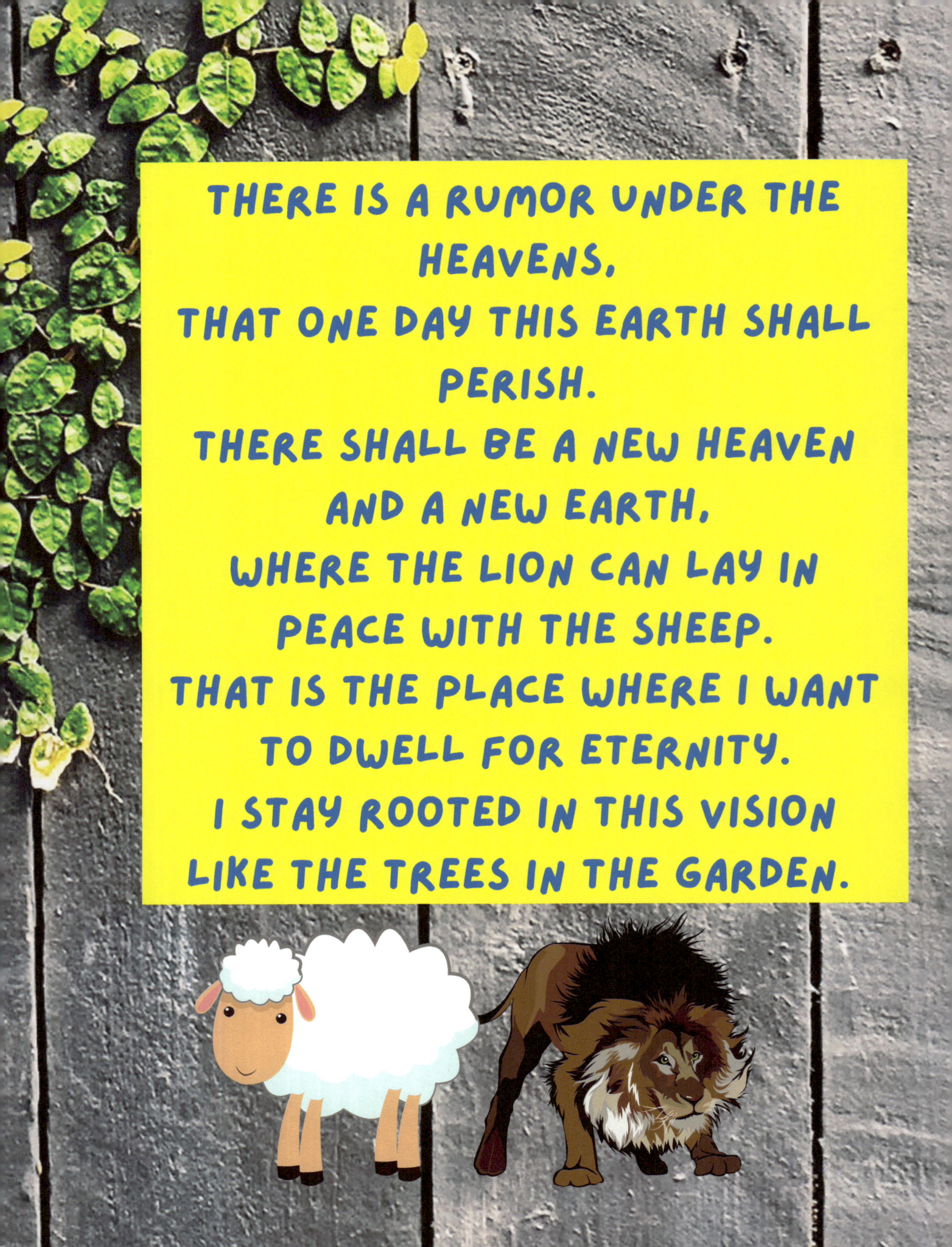

BE THE ACIDITY IN THE SODA BOTTLE,
BE THE ANSWER TO THE QUESTION.
BE THE LIGHT INSIDE THE TREACHEROUS TUNNEL,
BE THE QUESTION THAT INCITES THE SEARCH FOR AN ANSWER.
BE.

BE THE "US" WITHIN JUST,
BE THE "JUST" WITHIN JUSTICE.
STAND FIRM ON YOUR WORD,
EXIST WITHIN YOUR BELIEF.
BE LIKE THE OLD ROOTED TREE.
UNMOVABLE.

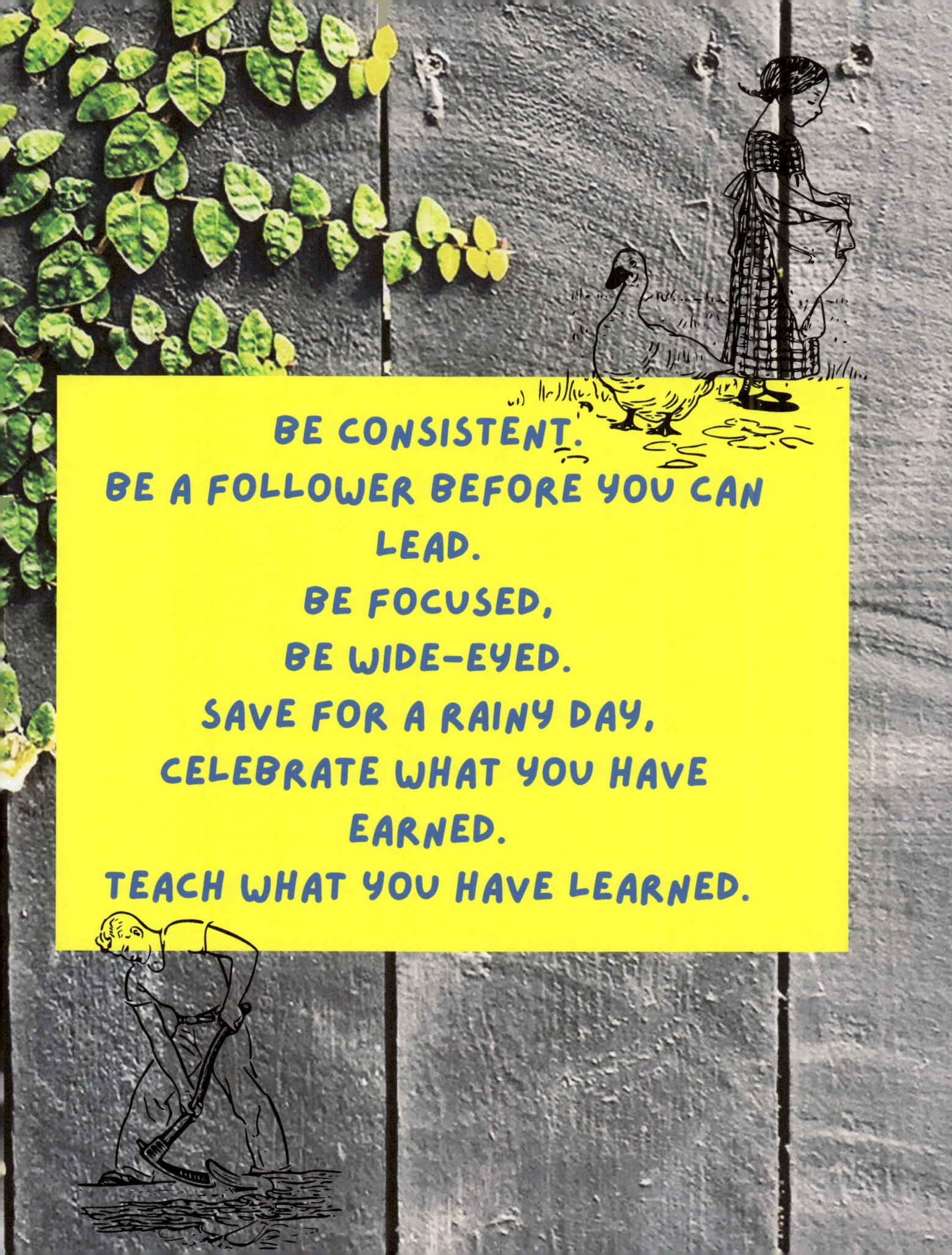

BE CONSISTENT.
BE A FOLLOWER BEFORE YOU CAN LEAD.
BE FOCUSED,
BE WIDE-EYED.
SAVE FOR A RAINY DAY,
CELEBRATE WHAT YOU HAVE EARNED.
TEACH WHAT YOU HAVE LEARNED.

Live off of the good soil, be a balance of human and spirit.
Be a good neighbor, be the best representation of your true being.
Be a site to see as the big rooted tree.

What a beautiful world that we live in,
What an awesome time to be alive.
Depression intercedes in the air,
The land is full of hurt, shame, poverty, and panic.
Crime sits on every corner.

Mankind has lost its faith in God.
Plowing through the corrupted fields searching for refreshing fruits and waters.
Only to find death and loneliness.
Where are the rooted trees?

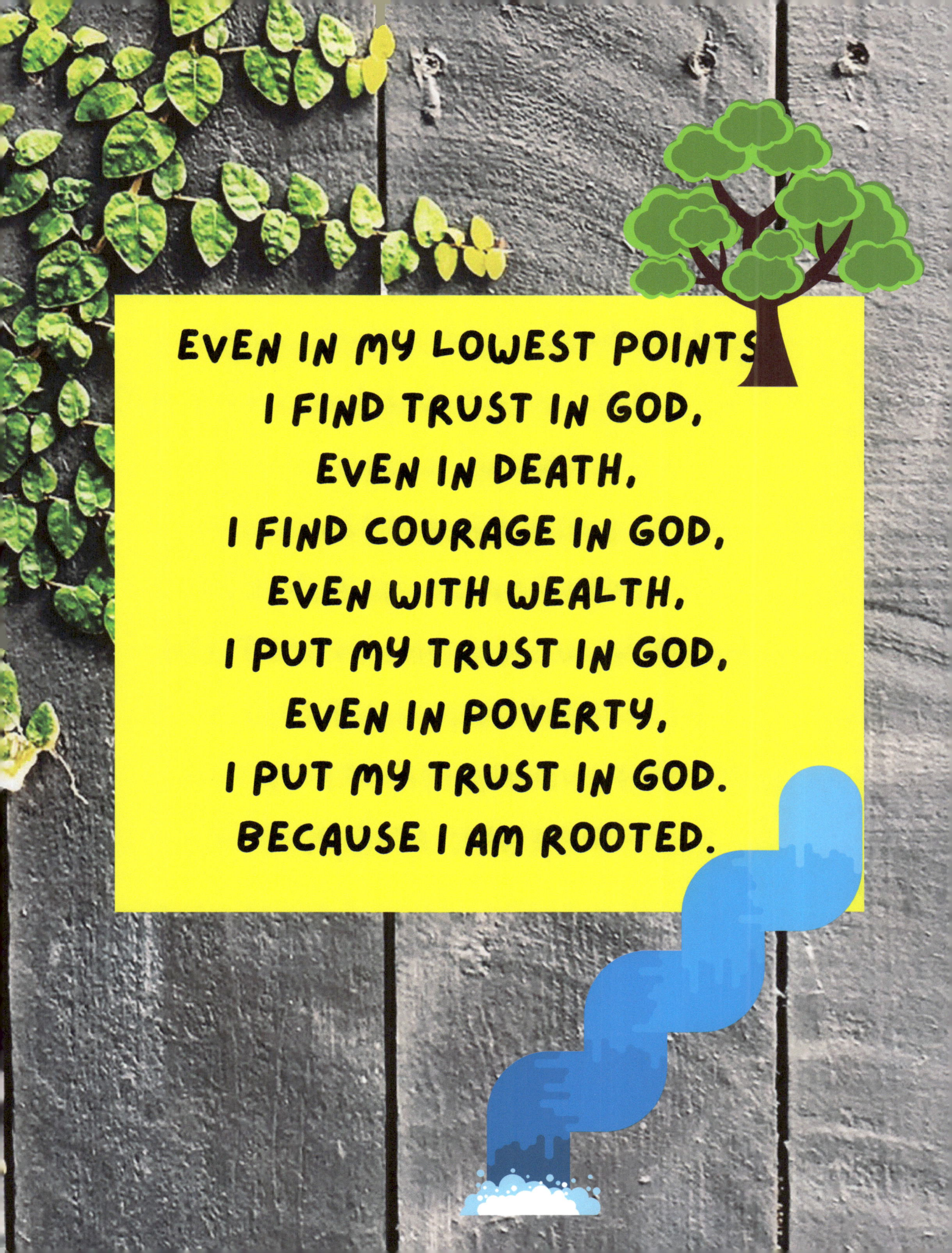

Though my stomach be filled with pain killers,
My blood still runs warm in a blizzard.
Though my faith be shaken on a daily,
I still remain rooted like the tree.
I will not let my fear remove my ambition.
I will remain unmoved.

BE A TREE THAT BEARS PLENTY OF FRUIT,
FULL OF NOURISHMENT AND WISDOM.
LET THE ANGELS ENCAMP AROUND YOUR GROUND,
STAND FIRM WITH CONFIDENCE.

Be sure to dream above the valleys,
Always think beyond the peaks.
But stay humble,
Remember where your core is.
It is interwoven within your roots.

Life is a gift,
Receive it gift wrapped or unboxed.
Protect what goes in your body.
Be conscious of what rolls off of your tongue.
Keep your heart pure,
And always stay rooted.
Just like the tree planted by the rivers of water.

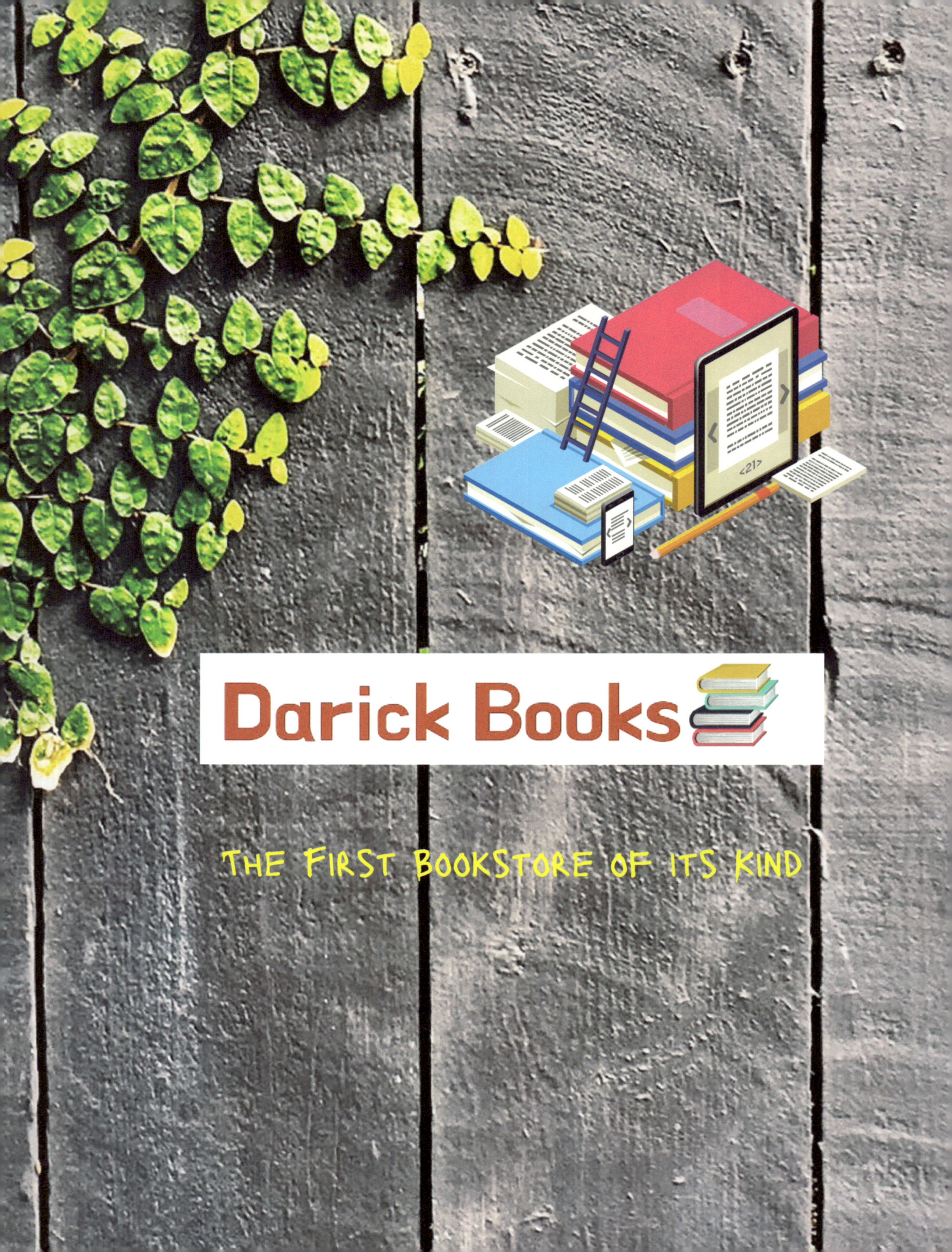

www.ingramcontent.com/pod-product-compliance
Lightning Source LLC
Chambersburg PA
CBHW042015150426
43196CB00003B/57